Driving the Lost Highway

By Jeff Weddle

UnCollected Press

Driving the Lost Highway
Copyright © 2023 by Jeff Weddle

All rights reserved. This book in full or partial form may not be used or reproduced by electronic or mechanical means without permission in writing from the author and UnCollected Press.

Cover Art:
DRIVING THE LOST HIGHWAY
JEFF WEDDLE

Book Design by:

UnCollected Press
8320 Main Street, 2nd Floor
Ellicott City, MD 21043

For more books by UnCollected Press:
www.therawartreview.com

First Edition 2023
ISBN: 979-8-9883022-6-1

Table of Contents

Rock on	1
The Truth About Cats	2
A Sudden Knocking	3
Or Gram Parsons	5
Home Now	7
Christmas with Nana	8
Not So Strange a Sight, If You Think About It	10
This Family	12
In Case You Wondered	14
We Could Be Heroes	15
Into the Wild	17
Worth a Thousand Words	19
Satori	21
Stormy Weather	22
d. a. levy	23
The Artist	24
Tonight in the City	25
A Talk with a Good One	27
Primate	30
Alchemical	31
Somewhere	32
Closing Time	33
A Luminous Manifestation	34
Remember Me?	35
Morning Sandwich	36
She Said, He Said	38
That Old Time Religion	39
Unless You are Jill or Diane di Prima	40
Just Your Standard Love Story	41
Listen to Me	43
Let Yourself Be	45
Messiah	46

Settled In	47
Yeeee Haaaaawwwwww	48
Gentlemen Prefer Blondes	49
Some Kind of Glory Hallelujah	50
The Essential Guide to Wine	51
Think of It as a Professional Conference	52
Spirit of America	53
Deity	54
Oh, Bother	55
Garage Sale	56
Sweet Hitchhiker	57
Reading Milosz at Midnight	59
Punk's Journey	61
Listen, Jill	62
This Beauty	63
Here's the 411	64
Not John James Audubon, Actually	65
Made for Each Other	68
It Might Have Been Tennessee	69
There's Poetry Somewhere, I guess	70
I am Just a Poe Boy, Though My Story's Seldom Told	71
Gus, Always	72
At the Bookstore	73
How to be a Poet	74
Things in the Rain	75
One Hundred Dollars a Day, Plus Expenses	76
In Some City	77
Anticipation	78
Down in the Keys	79
Papa	80
My Best Guess	81
Modern Romance	82
Please Be Considerate	83
This Particular Second	84
The Herd Lined Up	85
Manifesto	86

Advice to My Children	88
An Inadequate Poem for My Children	90
Incredible Coincidence. Incredible.	91
In This Place	93
Hit Parade	94
Hey, Sailor	95
Story of My Life	96
The Things We Do for Love	97
From the Get-Go	98
Here's My Advice	99
What's the Story, Morning Glory?	100
Poem for a Dear Lady	101
At Your Service	102
Driving the Lost Highway	103
So, Then?	105
My Wish	106
It's Just Business	107
The Night they Raided Minsky's	108
Pilgrimage	109

Always for Jill

Rock On

Everything
worth anything
is music.

Anything
worth everything
is rock and roll.

The Truth About Cats

It is just as you
have always
suspected:

Cats compose poems
in their heads
most all the time,
poems so beautiful
we could not
hear them
and survive.

But they are wise enough
in their indifferent love
never to share these poems
with those who
provide food

while dogs
poor things

think of nothing
but baseball
and magic
and don't give a damn
who knows.

A Sudden Knocking

Small killer with big dreams
her mind like the gears
of a forgotten music box
unloved and lost
in a hot attic.

Thoughtful assassin
not wanting you to suffer
(just a quick pop
then nothing)
used up and lost in tears
most eyes would never recognize.

Little shooter on the move.

Knives are fine in a pinch
or poison in a frosted glass.

Deft beauty out for blood
in the nicest way possible.

That's her at the door right now.
Do you answer?

She is quite lovely after all
and a brilliant conversationalist.

For reasons you will not understand,
you are her greatest ambition.

She will be loving, soft,
the one you have wished for,
and prepared for anything.

Consider well.

You have this final chance
and there are many worse ways
to go.

Or Gram Parsons

The quickest way to lose me
is to write about
a finch, a wren, or a snowy egret.

I mean, for fuck's sake.

Don't write about a sparrow
and expect me to be happy.

If it has to be about a bird,
make it about a penguin
or a chicken
or David Crosby
with his variant spelling.

Vultures are sometimes fine,
but for the love of God,
read the room.

The quickest way to wither
is to write about flowers, any sort.

Clouds,
sunshine,
dewy grass.

Shoot the flowers
out of a cannon, maybe.

Let them knock a bird
right out of the sky.

Let a cat be waiting.

That's the show.
That's how it's done.

Bye bye, birdie.

Home Now

Coffee in my favorite cup,
a rainy day,
with the family asleep
and Sasha
beside me
purring love.

This soft couch
is an old friend
telling us
our quiet stories

and I am astonished
that the world
does not concern itself
with my here
or my there
for a lovely second.

The road ahead
and the road behind,
like the crush of dwindling years,
will have to find patience.

Sasha is my knowing mistress
with her sweet demands
and my coffee
must not get cold.

Christmas with Nana

Of course you are here.

There are photographs:
You with Pa,
with Jill and Amy,
with the grandchildren.

Of course you are here.

After all it is Christmas
and no one loves Christmas
more than you.

You are the lights,
the ornaments,
the tall tree
that spills presents
in a tidy circle
around its base.

You are the bowl
of oyster crackers
and the Chex Mix
Amy will make later.

You are the way
the furniture
is arranged
in each room
and the voice
we all hear,
plain as day,

when we are still.

You sit beside me now
on this couch,
the same couch
where we sat that Sunday
when we stayed home from church
and watched the beginning
of *Lonesome Dove*,
held hands,
and talked about family.

Of course you are here
as we open presents,
smile, give thanks,

and nurse wounds
scattered like scraps
of brightly colored paper
around your empty chair.

Not So Strange a Sight, If You Think About It

The man with the stuffed unicorn
is no longer married.

He is mostly bald and a little fat.
The man, I mean.

The unicorn is pink and plush
with a single, white snowflake
in each of his coal black eyes,
and hooves that put you in mind
of mother of pearl.

He doesn't look like
you would expect, really.

The unicorn, I mean.

He looks more like a hippopotamus
with a festive horn
than a magical stallion.

The man looks exactly
as you would expect:
Lost and weary.

The man with the stuffed unicorn
no longer has a child.

He was a late addition,
but that meant he was treasured
all the more.

The unicorn, I mean.
But you could say the same for the child,

if that's what you want to talk about.

No one wants to talk about that, though.

His name was Samuel,
but no one ever wants
to talk about him at all.

His mother was Ruth.
The man with the unicorn's mother, I mean.
Samuel's mother was Lydia.

No one wants to talk about her, either.

The man with the stuffed unicorn
keeps walking. He keeps walking
until he is just gone.

No one notices.

The unicorn remains plush and beautiful,
and the man will not let him go,
but he will never have a home.

This Family

It is early, and the four of us
wander through
our morning routine,
my daughter,
the cat, the dog
and me.

I feed the cat and dog
while my daughter makes do
with teen angst and water.

As always, the cat, having eaten,
judges and finds me wanting.

She takes her time
gliding to another place
while the dog,
climbing back onto the couch,
does not find herself so superior.

She sighs and glances up at me
and I think, "Okay, old girl, okay.
Another morning. What now?"

The sun is up and
the school bus arrives
to take my daughter to a place
she mostly doesn't want to go.

The cat is somewhere secret
and the dog and I wait
for my wife to awaken
and come downstairs
for coffee.

She will tell the dog
to get off the couch,
perhaps say she loves us,
and stay quiet for a time
as morning fills her
and my daughter rides the bus
to a place she would rather not be.

Just for this moment,
I sit here with the dog, content,
knowing this
is as good as life allows.

The cat will reappear
and, in a few hours,
my daughter will return
from the place
she would mostly rather not be.

My wife will love me
and the dog will sigh and yawn
and chase rabbits in her sleep.

We will rest inside our tender blessings
and tomorrow will come
and the day after
and the day after that.

I am sure the cat, wherever she is,
understands everything.

In Case You Wondered

Needing to write
but you can't write
is like needing to cry
but you can't cry.

It's like being filled with love
and having no one
to give it to.

It's like the necessary death
that hasn't come
and the terror that it never will.

Needing to write
but you can't write
is the best dream
you never had:

Complete darkness
with a merciless star
desperate to explode

or rocks in your pockets
pulling you to the bottom
of the lake
as you open your lungs
to sing.

We Could be Heroes

After they murdered Kong,
the flyboys went out for beer.

"What a day," Larry said
to no one in particular.
"Did you see that damned thing?
Big as a damned department store."

"Can department stores
really be damned?" asked Reggie,
the twin brother
of Larry's ex-wife, Maud.

Reggie looked so much like Maud
that Larry sometimes felt
uncomfortable urges,
which he disguised with sadistic mocking.

"You're missing the point," said Bernard,
in his interrupting way.

"Which is?" countered Reggie.

"Which is that we killed
a big motherfucking ape
and we should already be famous
and draped with dames."

There was general agreement,
with even Larry wishing
some broad would sass her way over
for a chance to fuck a Kong killer.

No such luck.

Across the sea, a gigantic,
radioactive dinosaur awoke
from a ten-thousand-year slumber.

None of them knew it yet,
but they would all be dead in a week.

"Yes, they can," said Larry,
answering Reggie's question
from what seemed an age past.
"Well, haunted anyway.
That's just as good."

Into the Wild

The limp of the tiger
stalking the ragged ape
under a dying moon.

Nothing lasts.

Even the kudu understand.

They don't run.
They don't even skitter.

The limp of the tiger,
the puzzle of a dead man
beside a dirt road,

a man roaring
just yesterday.

His woman will never know
the truth.

The ragged ape
turns to face the tiger,
sizing up the limp.

In a small house
miles away
a woman
who does not yet know
she is a widow
makes hard love
to a boy half her age.

Everything is vicious.

The boy basks in his good fortune
as the ape continues on its way
and the tiger gives up
and looks for a place to sleep
away from the beaten path.

Waking up
or sleeping forever,
each is just the same.
The tiger is ready for what comes.

The widow screams in ecstasy.

The boy believes he
understands something
he had not known before,
but he is wrong.

Love is a possibility
but, as even the most ragged ape
will tell you, a good death
is less certain

and definitely matters more.

Worth a Thousand Words

The oldest surviving photograph
of a woman
is in a box in an attic.

It has been seen only twice,
once by its photographer,
who developed it,
put it in a box
and, soon after, died.

The box was stored in an attic
by the photographer's jealous wife,
who was the only other person to see it.

The wife was not the woman
in the photograph.

Though the woman
in the photograph
was not beautiful,
it is quite a beautiful
photograph.
Such was the genius
of the photographer.

That house will burn tonight,
taking everything.

The woman's bones
are in the ground,
as are the photographer's bones
and those of his jealous,
and quite beautiful, wife,

but the model's face,
though forgotten in an attic,
is still with us
until the house
is consumed by fire.

When it is gone,
no one will know or care.
The fire will be remembered
for silly reasons.
No one will ever know
what was lost.

Satori

The boundless child,
eternal in the dying grass,
is intent upon the infinite ant.
She has forgotten
the tomorrow she creates.

The ant,
fixed upon the pleasures
of the queen,
understands everything
but what the child believes.

The dog could not care less.
He concerns himself with the cat
and her dreams of pigeons,
and sees clearly
that love is the first canvas.

This comedy
is both sphere
and vapor.

Like the bright leaves of autumn,
it is here for a moment
and gone.

Stormy Weather

Severe weather has been detected
in the vicinity of Edna St. Vincent Millay
and odd, beautiful trash shares the wind
with a circling hawk,
or maybe it's a falcon.

Ask Yeats,
he might know.

It can be quite a surprise
how a small, yellow bag
can change the course
of a poem,

as hurricane force words
rain down on parched sidewalks
and even Sylvia Plath seeks shelter,
because fear is a many dimensional street.

Sometimes it's better to stay home
and other times you'll live longer
if, brave or not, you run straightaway
into the storm.

d. a. levy

An earthbound angel of long ago
took a bullet for the world
and heaven got that much sweeter.

Can we now say "Screw Cleveland,"
knowing how he loved that town
even as it dogged him to the grave?

A beat angel took one
right between the eyes
leaving his gashed absence
to stand for all the poems
he never wrote,

to maybe show what he meant
by the poems he got on paper,

the things he wrote for tomorrow
or just himself
while sleeping
with the old-eyed muse.

Can we now say
we might love Cleveland
for his sake?

Can we say,
"d. a., thanks
for coming, man"?

The Artist

What a beautiful man he was,
with his ginger hair and black eyes,
the words pouring from his hands like honey.

What a beautiful man who never spoke,
could not dance,
and was unknown to the world.

What a beautiful man with secret pages
holding the blood of days.

No one knew he was here
and when he left
there wasn't the slightest ripple.

His beauty lasts forever,
untouched and pure,
in the great vacuum of time,

a riot of flowers
in a world of killing weeds.

Tonight in the City

Palsied wing walkers prowling dark streets
looking for degraded romance.

Painfully thin children singing brilliant songs
in an unknown, dead language,
their dark eyes shining.

Beautiful women with greasy hair
and hard souls withholding mercy.

It's going rain. Everyone knows it's coming.

Artists in oil and watercolor battling
smug sidewalk caricaturists.

Sculptors in clay hurrying to
their busboy jobs
in trafficky downtown twilight.

No one holds back tears any more.
That's one thing we have.

High winds and hail big as baseballs.

U-boats dolled up for New Year's Eve
and everybody gets a kiss.

Windows smashed. Floods.

The prophecy of flight only a punchline
to an overly complex joke.

Blood pooling in odd places
for no apparent reason.

This extravaganza is closing.

Tickets go for a song, since
the reviews are bitter as lost stones
in a middling cherry pie.

Please smother me
with your approximate love.

Kiss my face while you can.

A Talk with a Good One

Of course I read Bukowski
when I was young.
Everyone did, I guess,
but the good ones always stopped
after a while.

Richard told me I had a fierce line
in my new poem
and it reminded him of Roethke.

I was a drinker, too,
sometimes a couple,
maybe even three beers a night,
the bad influence of Buk.

His friends called him that,
but I don't know how he had friends.
Right?

That went on for years,
all through college.
Of course I switched to wine
when I was accepted here.
Mostly a good red.

I can finish off an entire bottle
in three or four days
and I guess it should worry me,
but that's the life of a poet, right?

Richard said he drank absinthe in Paris,
but had to stop
because everyone knew
Hemingway drank it in the twenties

and Hemingway is such a bore.

Maybe I'll switch to scotch.

Hannah is tightening up her thesis,
you know.
She showed it to me last week.
One of the poems is going to be
in the *Georgia Review*!
Can you imagine?

Richard told me I should submit to *Poetry*.
He went to school with an editor
and can get me through the slush pile.

He said my poems sometimes
remind him of Pound
and sometimes of Adrianne Rich,
so I guess I'm in touch
with the feminine.

Richard runs the best seminar
in the workshop, don't you think?
Everyone says so.

You still want to talk about Bukowski?
Whatever for?

I outgrew him a long time ago.

Richard said he read a few
Bukowski poems
when he was young
and knew right away

the man was a joke,
and that's just a fact.

You'll see it eventually.
The good ones always do.

Primate

I'm a smart monkey
with my jibber-jabber
and my hooky-hoo.

I'm a smart monkey
with my tin cup
and my crazy dance.

I'm a smart monkey
god damn it.

I'm a smart monkey
so you'd better watch
your banana stash.

I'm a smart monkey.

I see things
you miss
and sometimes
I watch you sleep.

I'm a smart monkey
and I'm packing heat
right along with
my jibber-jabber
and hooky-hoo.

I'm a smart monkey.
How about you?

Alchemical

Milosz dealt with vodka and gold.
Foolish.

I suggest gin and silver.
Radiant moon

and precious drunken silver.
Drunken people in their stately clothing.

Vodka and gold are tacky,
as everyone knows.

Silver flashing into the promise
of time.

Nothing is empty
because we all live inside.

The distance between stars is the big con.
It is so easy to be lost,
almost comforting.

Gin helps a little.

We are base
and easily transmuted.

Magic words, like magic beans,
fool most everyone.

Surely Milosz would agree.

Somewhere

I like to think Eric Cash
still wanders the earth
and his ghost bones
are made of stories
and his ghost breath
is made of poems.
His old van is long gone
but he wouldn't need it now.
Old ghost compadre
of pool halls
and beer-soaked days,
the world was never
all you wanted.
How could it be?
You had a good cat, Elvis,
and if he were still here
he'd tell us all
that you were electric,
a kind heart against the odds,
funny as hell
and gone too soon,
but you shook things up
for a while.

Closing Time

Dean used to say, at closing time,
"You don't have to go home
but you can't stay here."

And now Dean's gone
off to heaven,
so that place sure
got a whole lot livelier,

with all the saints
and Eric Cash there
to make him welcome
with their big, angel hugs.

What a sight
that must have been.
Everyone back slapping
with goofy laughs
and the best old stories
made new.

We all go somewhere,
one way or another.

Now, Dean's where
the toasts go on and on
and Happy Hour
lasts forever.

Big, tender bear.
Friend.
Bartender for the ages.

I raise my glass to you.

A Luminous Manifestation

Find Isadora somewhere
between the dance
and the scarf,

the last flight
caught on celluloid
before the frames
end.

Her body in its smooth affinity
with air and water.

Her hard triumph
which seems so easy,
the kinetics of joy.

It is tragic,
the music of things,

the final days.
We mourn

those things undone
we are given
to remember.

But still,
the dance.

Remember Me?

We are different,
so why should I ask?
You take your coffee black,
and I take my with spite.

Accepted theory maintains
that there are books
and then there are stories.
I know which one you are not,
and am working on myself.

Here now: Tripping down the sidewalk
in memory
is better than freezing in tonight's rain.

You would call it a drizzle
but, then again, you are safe.

Sidewalks are harder
than you might believe.
So are open skies and cloud cover.

I might ask anyway. Old time's sake
and all that.

What's the worst thing
that could happen?
The very worst, I mean.

Perhaps we'll find out,
but I don't think either of us
really want to know.

Morning Sandwich

I sit here eating a peanut butter sandwich
and drinking coffee with whole milk.

It's one of those days.

Got too drunk last night,
but just beer, thank God.

People kept walking by the bar
and yelling up at me.

I was sitting on the deck
and I was drunker than a snake
and people kept coming by
or yelling up: "*Jeff! Jeff!*"

And I yelled back or raised my bottle
and sat there as the faces came and went.

It was one of those nights.

It had rained all day
and the streets glowed black
and the tables and chairs were soaked
and I sat there and sat there
and I kept thinking: *Is this it?*
Is this the best moment?

as a breeze whispered across the night
and tickled my face, my hands, my hair.

And I sit here now with my coffee,
peanut butter and bread,
as gray sunlight limps into my room.

I toast the night, the rain,
hot, steaming coffee,
you,
each tender,
small moment.

She Said, He Said

She said, "Pretend I'm dead."
She said, "Pretend I'm cold to the touch."
"Baby," he said, "you're crazy."
She said, "My skin feels like old mayonnaise
and my internal organs itch."
She said, "I want you to watch me sleeping
when I don't know you're there."
"Baby," he said, "you're a fun chick."
She said, "I have a disease and your face is its name."
She said, "Scoot over. You're hogging the blanket."
"Baby," he said, "I want to coat you in popcorn oil
and use you for a slip 'n' slide."
She said, "Everyone is wicked
but some are more skilled than others."
She said, "In my world there are no kangaroos."
"Baby," he said, "I don't give a fuck about kangaroos."
She said, "I do."
He said, "I do, too."
They kissed.
And they lived happily ever after.

That Old Time Religion

Old people who find Jesus
and want to tell you about it
are the worst.

They go on and on
so you'll know they're pious as can be
and maybe Jesus will count that
in the balance of their good works
and their bad,

or at least you will know
they are truly holier than you are,
and that makes them happy.

Hell's waiting for everybody, anyway.
In fact, we are already there.

The doddering and newly righteous
are proof of that.

Don't expect anything more,
no matter what some old fool
tells you, fire in his eye

and tomato soup stains,
like the blood of the lamb,
decorating his hideous rayon shirt.

Unless You are Jill or Diane di Prima

Sure, you've probably
done cool things
in your life,
but did you ever convince
a beautiful young girl
to go to a costume party
dressed as Diane di Prima?

Well, I did.

Then I convinced her
to marry me.

You think you're cool?
Top that.

Yes, yes, I know, *she*
already topped it
when she went
to a costume party
dressed as Diane di Prima.

Fair enough.
I can't touch that.

But, unless you're
the hippest chick
in nine states
and goddess of all you survey,
neither can you.

Just Your Standard Love Story

He said,
"Some of us
would be happy
just to see
a flying saucer
a real one
you know
from outer space
and shit.
I know I would."

She nodded,
not listening,
thinking instead
of old lovers
who didn't
give a fuck
about flying saucers
and shit
but who had
for a while
given a fuck
about her.

That was
their way

until the afternoon
she answered
a knock
at the front door
and three men
dressed all in black

and looking
very much
like old lovers
took her
far, far away

and he never knew
where she went
or suspected
the unending
pleasures
she endured
at way past
light speed
and accelerating

but he did still wonder
what became
of their love
and, more specifically,
of her

though he never
saw her again

and he never saw
a flying saucer either

and that's just
sad as hell.

Listen to Me

Don't let yourself get old,
but if you must get old,
don't let yourself get crazy.
If you get crazy,
don't let yourself get mean.
If you get mean,
don't be surprised
to find that love
only goes so far
before you find
yourself alone.
Old, crazy, mean and alone
is about as shitty as it gets
until, of course, it gets worse
and it always
always
always
gets worse.
So, buck up.
Get your exercise.
Eat right.
Pray, if you believe in that sort of thing.
Do what it takes, right now.
Tomorrow is right around the corner
and the day after that
then another
and it all comes rushing.
Don't let yourself get old.
I don't know what else to tell you
except that the world finally swallows
everyone.
We all know this,
and it is very sad.
Sometimes the swallowing is fast

but, more often,
it goes slowly,
too slowly for anyone
to bear.

Let Yourself Be

The world will fool you if you let it
and you might as well.

The bliss of the trick
has sustained many
who deserved less.

The blue sky.
The white clouds.
God's green Earth.

Check, check, and check.

Not gifts, just illusions on loan
from blind nature.

Then there is the trick of love,
even romance, if you are lucky.

Take it all.

The world doesn't care,
but that is not important
if you get your hour of hope
before everything is exposed.

The truth is always too awful.
You might as well forget about it
and glide slowly to the grave.

Give in to the dream,
phony and sweet.

Love it while you can.

Messiah

A man alone. Much hustle and bustle.
The town clock might chime any minute.
Hands in pockets.
Heavy overcoat.
Overcast. No rain.
Not just yet.
A man walking along a sidewalk.
People everywhere.
A man alone with his thoughts.
Car horns honk. Someone laughs.
A woman. Someone cries.
A child. Someone runs.
The man. He runs
with no destination.
He runs and runs,
drenched with sweat.
He runs and runs.
The clock doesn't chime.
He runs and runs and runs.
Lightning splits the sky.
Thunder.
The people go about their day.
Hustle and bustle
minus one
who is finally and forever gone.
No one cares.
They have places to be.
No one understands
a damned thing.

Settled In

Another night in the lost motel
and now I believe
there are ghosts.

Maybe it's just me.

It seems like I've only been here since yesterday,
but that would make this....

I can't think about that now.

But I'm sure there is a ghost here,
at least one.

The creaking in the hall gives it away.

The odd stains that come and go.
The stench.
The conversations in the dark.

Another night in the lost motel.

Occasional headlights on a two-lane road,
and what wouldn't I give
for a bottle of decent bourbon?

I'm not singing
but I hear it
in the rooms,

tuneless and awful, unceasing,

telling me the mysteries
just the same.

Yeeee Haaaaawwwww

Old-souled girls who love polka bands
and cosmic dance floors
way out in the imagination.
Flying snakes. (Yes, that's a thing.)
Dizzy matrons filled with liquid dreams.
Redheads and blondes of long ago
with their bell bottoms and macramé tops
and nothing underneath.
Their good weed.
Brunettes of forever.
Clay pots buried for ten thousand years
that could answer all the questions
we are too silly to ask.
Flying spiders. (Also a thing.)
Good sports and dead friends.
Hammers ashamed of smashing.
Zombies and mules and the trauma of birth,
all these decades gone by.
Ghost rockets above Scandinavia.
Ghost trains in the darkness.
UFOs too shy for the White House lawn.
Zany dreams we mispronounced as "love."
Old-souled girls with their beautiful eyes.
Ask anyone worth knowing:
Polkas are fun as hell.
The party doesn't last forever.
Get out there and dance.

Gentlemen Prefer Blondes

Marilyn Monroe's breasts
were made of celluloid and sweat.
Her hair was spun from the marrow
of every sad boy's dream.
There's no way to know about her legs,
unless you really knew about her legs,
when they carried her
from one disappointment to the next
and to the one after that.
That's how spectacular they were.
Marilyn's face was the face
of an ancient wound and her radiant tummy
rested above the vault of heaven.
Her bottom was wiser than the sages,
her toes more musical than a French flute
and twice as noble.
Marilyn was most real when it came to soul.
She was aware that she was God,
just as she was aware
that she was damned.
She was likewise aware that oblivion
is our best reward.
At the end of the day,
celluloid and sweat
were her most enduring features.
But we should never forget her eyes.
Eyes like that are a preview to eternity.

Some Kind of Glory Hallelujah

Wasted on poetry and acid,
Budweiser victories on small town
sidewalks, dreaming
of dark-haired girls
and something better than love,
trying to find how to walk
the dream into waking
when real life didn't even mean shit.
Weed and whiskey and late nights
wandering in the woods,
late night howling
and getting down the lines
with the moon
burning angels in my pocket.
Words were everything
but I threw away my hours
with visions of beauty and the flesh,
with pool games and pitchers
and all the friends coming and going,
all of us heroes to empty dreams.
The words cut hard
and I was the best of pretenders,
long haired Romeo Zero
with nothing to show for nothing
but, Jesus, how I loved to strut.

The Essential Guide to Wine

Being within the dead,
that sweet wine
was no longer magic.
Poets had no use
for wine inside the corpse
even of a friend
or even of a beautiful woman.
The dead, that is, killed man's first wine,
rendering it moot.
The wine that mattered
rested in forgotten cellars,
in oaken casks older than the world.
It dreamed its own sweet dreams
and fought occasional nightmares.
All who would someday die
were warned away,
forbidden to know its blessings,
an immortality never offered,
a gift never shared.

Think of It as a Professional Conference

Plath and Bukowski
sharing daddy issues in Heaven (Our father who art wicked
who art shame, our father who art
a mother fucker.) Bukowski and Plath
sharing bourbon shots
and making up dirty limericks
to embarrass Pound later
when they would roust him for wilding.
Bukowski giving Plath
fatherly advice
while ogling her legs
and Plath playing the coquette.
(There once was a poet named Hank,
whose verses were terribly frank....) Oh, stop that.
Bukowski suggesting a three-way
with Dorothy Parker.
Plath hanging on Bukowski's
every word
and spitting in his drink
when he turns his head.
Bukowski with deep scars.
Plath with deep regret.
Oh, the babies they would make
if they were able.
What a party. What fire.
All the beauty and explosion
and the rare, fine words gone mad.

Spirit of America

The man with the violin
stands with his sign
in the grocery parking lot.
He is small and brown
and very serious about his playing,
which is quite beautiful.
The man with the violin is a single father,
or that's what the sign says.
He has a hat on a chair to collect tips.
The shoppers come and go.
The sign says he is playing
to provide for his kids.
The lovely music floats
above the people
going into and out of the store.
No one looks at the man
or puts anything in his hat.
The shoppers have many things to do.
It is almost Thanksgiving, after all,
and the day,
like these good, Christian people,
is so very cold.

Deity

The child remembered being
the wild god of the world,
being Jeffers' hawk,
the icy thrill of flight,
even above a burning forest.
The child felt this in his blood,
even more than in memory.
But the child did not understand
his own meaning
and, thus, believed everyone
was a wild god,
as wild and all powerful as he,
and so said nothing,
just happy to live
in a splendid world
of titans and apple trees,
a creek behind his house,
and the sweet cherry pies
his mother made
when someone's birthday
rolled around,
and other special days
or every so often
when she thought of her boy
or just got the urge.

Oh, Bother

Each one Christopher Robin
for a while,
all of us Alice.
Down the rabbit hole
and into the wood.
Back again
to forget and forget.

Garage Sale

Silent man, late forties,
behind a table
covered with things
that should not be
for sale.

Noisy woman, a bit younger,
in charge.
She knows it's time
for everything to go.

Their future must be clean,
like nothing ever happened.

She would sell the trophies
but they are no more
in demand
than photographs
of a child gone fishing,
empty closets
or someone else's socks.

It is all too much,
these trinkets
and chains,

the broken puzzle
of a dead
American family.

Sweet Hitchhiker

Old car on its last legs,
tired driver, night blind and lost,
lights from small houses as you cruise
the two-lane road,
bedroom lights and living rooms,
porch lights,
and you imagine
what is happening inside.

Laughter, joy, paranoia,
blank faces staring at televisions,
staring at walls,
or looking across a kitchen table
at eyes that once meant home
but are now an uninteresting mystery.

Evil thoughts and beatings,
apathy.

Bathtubs overflowing
because someone got drunk
and forgot to turn off the water.

Electric bills two months past due
and no milk in the refrigerator.

Crying babies, crying women,
men all used up
with no choice but to go on.

Maybe, here and there,
the possibility of hope.

Five beers left from a twelve pack

and something good on the radio.

The pretty hitchhiker
glares from beside the road
and is clearly trouble
but you pick her up anyway,
in your old car with bad shocks,
bald tires and no spare

and the real story begins.

Reading Milosz at Midnight

I flip the pages looking
for shorter poems
because I'm lazy
and also because
I write shorter poems,
also because I'm lazy.

There's one about
his wife's cremation
and their marriage troubles
and how they stuck it out.

And there's one about a blacksmith
and flames.

The old boy had a thing for fire, it appears.

My mind wanders to a day
when I watched a Kentucky mule
hitched to a press
trudge in an endless circle
to crush sugar cane.

My mind wanders to young Paula Hinchman,
her colorful skirt billowing in the wind,
unaware that I saw her,
and me thinking how pretty
that girl was
before I realized it was she
who broke my heart a dozen times
with a dozen more heartbreaks to come.

I flip through his pages
and I flip through my pages.

I'm sure that mule is long dead
and Paula is old now, like me.

Some of the poems go on
and on and on. How tiresome.

Nothing is true but what we can touch,
so poems, like this, might as well be ghosts.

Punk's Journey

It's nobody's business
why you are crying
and everything, everywhere
is a hard minute late.

You howl, of course,
like you stole the devil's lungs

knowing that somewhere
the moon is shining

somewhere the planets
give away their secrets

and somewhere the girl
you will someday meet
is maybe dancing
or reading a novel

a thousand miles away,
next door,
or at the dark end of an alley,

perhaps buying odd weapons
for odd reasons
or shy and in need,

like the beautiful orchid
the blind man did not pick,

dumb luck,

and forever
your maddest love.

Listen, Jill

I never promised myself
that I would sit alone,
writing poems
in a Paris cafe,
or drink absinthe
with a bohemian girl
in a dangerous bar,
say 1:00 a.m.,
at the end of a blind alley.
I never promised myself
I would watch the sunrise
from atop a remote mountain
or run with the bulls in Spain
or hitchhike across the country
searching for kicks
or the pearl of enlightenment.
I never promised myself
money or fame.
All I promised myself
was I would find you,
somewhere in the world,
and I did.

This Beauty

She was pretty
in the style of the day,

with the eyes, lips, hair,
all done to fit the rules,

and she was nice
when the moment demanded

and often petty
in the sly manner
of women of the day,

sometimes mean, even cruel,

but she was pretty
by anyone's standards
if the standards fit
the rules of the day.

She had the eyes,
the lips, the hair,

all of it,

and she was adored
by those who loved the rules
often petty as they were

in the style of eyes, lips, hair,
all done up pretty

all done up in the sly manner
of women of the day.

Here's the 411

This thing is dead.
Don't touch it.

This thing is hard to love,
though some say they do.

If you get close enough
you will understand,
but stay back.

This thing is dead and also lonely.

You have no idea
of the places
you might be hidden away.

This thing is dead
but does not mind so much.

Forget you were ever here.

Don't touch it.
There will be no other warning.

Not John James Audubon, Actually

The painter of birds
painted birds
and only birds
and took pride
in the exact nature
of his paintings.

He painted birds at rest and in flight,
birds nesting, birds walking on the ground,
birds in battle with their insecurities,
birds fighting with other birds,
birds hunting prey,
birds in their death throes,
birds inside tornadoes,
birds with broken hearts,
birds perched on telephone wires,
birds in abject confusion,
birds with one eye gone,
birds dancing,
birds in love,
and birds breaking free of eggs.

He painted birds of all sorts:
Falcons, eagles, chickens, ducks,
wrens, ravens, crows, penguins,
puffins, dodos, sparrows,
Madagascar pochards,
doves, emus, swallows,
flamingos, gulls, pelicans,
ostriches, geese,
redwing blackbirds,
hummingbirds, pigeons,
parrots, tufted nuthatches, macaws,
myna birds, canaries and so forth.

He painted every sort of bird
except snowy egrets
because he had his standards, didn't he?

The painter of birds
was meticulous in his work,
down to the last detail
of the smallest feather,
though only he saw his birds for what they were.
Others saw broken lamps
and exhausted truck drivers
eating three-egg omelets
in cheap but clean diners,
mud pies,
epic poems composed in small apartments
at 3:00 a.m.,
still lifes with roses,
nude women well past their prime,
rocket ships to Jupiter,
pimento cheese sandwiches,
couches with dirty cushions,
lost men down to their last cigarette,
movie theater marquees
advertising forgotten flops,
empty bourbon bottles,
pungent incense,
serial killers coming in third in spelling bees
and celebrating,
torch singers, tears, backhoes, clowns,
radishes, television comedies,
aikido masters with their smirks,
shotguns,
bowling trophies,

crack pipes,
treasure maps,
prostitutes enjoying their job,
graham crackers and mist.

Things like that.

The painter of birds was a simple man,
so no one expected it
when he took flight
and headed straight into the sun,
exploding into supernova
and modern dance,
though it would be wrong
to say anyone was truly surprised.

His paintings were all he left behind.
I'm sure you've seen them in your dreams
and have died a little in their presence.
Holy things do this to commoners like us.
You will see them again, be certain.
Avert your gaze as needed.

Made for Each Other

Lyn Lifshin and Octavio Paz
on an outing in late Autumn.
Terse and rambling
together in a bouquet.

Words drip from the air
like ice cream
melting in the sun.

He kisses her hand. She blushes,
a schoolgirl for a moment,
and licks his eyes.

Luckily, his reflexes are good.

They embrace, naked,
beside a busy street.
Everything is exactly
as you imagine.

The odd lovers know you
despite yourself
and invite your gaze.

They draw you in
like rare fruit.
They are perfectly
delicious.

It might have been Tennessee

If I could remember
where we were
maybe it would all
come clear.

There was a room,
of course.
Inexpensive motel, but clean.

That's how we were.

All I remember is
the daylight,
you arriving in one car,
me in another.

It was afternoon, I think,
when we left.

I drove one way,
you took a different road.

We eventually
ended up somewhere.

Maybe it was home.

There's Poetry Somewhere, I Guess

There's poetry in a ragged hitchhiker
but my daughter forgot
her contact lenses
and I have to run them by her school.

There's poetry in a ragged hitchhiker,
but my wife wants to talk
about her new boss
and he's kind of funny looking.

There's poetry in a ragged hitchhiker,
but my dog needs a treat
and she's a very good dog.

There's poetry in a ragged hitchhiker,
but I really need to fix myself some eggs
and dry toast
because that's what's in the house.

There's poetry in a ragged hitchhiker,
but it's so chilly outside.

There's poetry in a ragged hitchhiker,
or at least I think I read that somewhere.

There's poetry in a ragged hitchhiker
but that will have to wait.

There's no time for poetry
and no one cares.

I have to run to the store for dog treats
and bacon, maybe butter for the toast,
and no riders are allowed.

I am Just a Poe Boy
Though My Story's Seldom Told

Sometimes I get confused.

Was it Annabel Lee
who had that raven?

Lenore hated the damned thing,
that's for sure.

Yeah, we had a kingdom by the sea.
Who didn't back then?

Of course, we were
never more
than kids.

Birds and sea kingdoms
were plenty for us,
as good as it got.

But we always said
we'd summer
down past
the mountains of the moon
and we never did.

That's my one regret.

Gus, Always

On the first night of the world
I held you and we cried.

You were cold
and I was tired beyond reason.

On the first night your mother slept,
exhausted

and I got up on the hour
again and again
with your cries.

On the first night of the world
we knew nothing.

We were terrified.
Elated.

We didn't see the last night coming.
We didn't see you packed and ready.
We did not know how hard it would be.

After all, it was so many years away.

On the last night, I held your mother
and we cried.

We were filled with you
and heavy with memories.

We shivered, not cold,
just overcome with love.

At The Book Store

My knees ache
and I am tired
in this crush of holiday shopping
but, before I go, I must buy
The Poetry of Pablo Neruda
and a Zen garden for Harper.
The poetry, for now, is for me,
but I won't be surprised
if she claims it down the road.
That kid. Brilliant. Quite a handful.
All love and forward motion.
Was I ever such a force?
No. I can say that plainly.
The Zen garden is a small
Christmas present she hinted for
the last time we were here.
I told her no, but she probably
didn't believe me.
Like I said, brilliant,
though I hope she will still
be surprised.
Either way,
I will be an old man
and will read the Neruda
while it is still mine to read,
and she will be fresh and young,
my brilliant daughter,
all fierce love and forward motion,
and she will tend her garden.

How to Be a Poet

Alone is not so bad
if you have a nice bar to visit
and drink a few beers,
watch the young girls flirt with
the bartender.
Alone is fine
if you have enough
salted peanuts
and a notebook
that feels good in your hand,
and a pen with plenty of ink.
Alone is the way to be
if the words decide to come.
The bartender can water
the potted plants.
The girls can laugh
at the old man
watching
from the shadows.
The words can laugh
at us all.

Things in the Rain

Jimmy, who sleeps on the corner,
says the sidewalk
only forgives
the dead.
I think he's an optimist.

What I would give for a bottle,
a pack of smokes,
a ticket to yesterday.

It was mostly in her eyes
and the rest was in her perfume.
I lost the only photograph I had
and can't find anyone
who remembers.

Her voice was like a crisp c-note
won on a last chance bet.
Nothing forgives.
A mystery like her
is best left be.

One Hundred Dollars a Day, Plus Expenses

The doomed femme fatale,
classic art.
Holy aspiration of gutted Hollywood.
Dark hair, haunted eyes, silk blouse,
cigarettes.
Footsteps echo on a blind street
as dim light escapes
a third story window.
Maybe you're careful,
but not careful enough.
The two of you carved up cleanly
and buried in the desert
is as likely as the two of you
sipping whisky in a dark bar.
Jealousy is the only trump to greed.
A trusted revolver at arm's reach
and one empty chamber.
It's all for love,
but never mind.
Love and two bits
is barely enough to get you
into her bed, her cold heart,
and hung up
in the inevitable double cross.

In Some City

I am here for the living street,
a small gang of pretty girls,
each of them golden,
cats in hiding and sizing up the day,
ice cream dropped on the sidewalk
by a screaming child,
a young mother in a blue cotton shift,
half angry, half distracted
by a sale in the dress shop window.
Smell the exhaust from five hundred cars
rolling by just in the last hour.
Over there is the hotdog man.
Look the other way and it's a punk
in beat leather and her big poet dreams.
An empty wine bottle in a brown bag
tells stories only the angels can hear.
Give me the living street
and keep the dying remains.
It's half past three and night is still a dream.
Everything has a chance.

Anticipation

One day, I will be young.
I will be supple
and filled with wonder.
Old ladies will pinch my cheek
and offer me unwrapped peppermints
from their purses.
I will eat these without a care.
Maybe I will also get a dog. I hope I do.
We might walk together in the woods
or sit in my room, just the two of us,
and dream our perfect dreams.
One day I will be vapor.
And then stone.
But just for a day, I will be young.
I will count all the stars and forget.
The next day will come.

Down in the Keys

Young man on Hemingway's wall,
rowdy Key West night.
His intent, beyond getting
to the other side,
is unclear,
but the wine explains most of it.
Jeans rip in the climb
and he is caught by a guard
who sends him on his way.
These things are heavy
with imagined portent.
Later, he will drink at the tourist bars
and, being stupid and drunk,
spit over a balcony railing,
run from a certain beating,
and somehow escape.
The young man believes
he will soon write of these things.
He decides this will be fine
and will worry
about the hangover
tomorrow.

Papa

We return to Hemingway for the death,
too much of it, in the beautiful hills,
the bluest sky.
We come back for the poetry
that no one else saw.
Love, too,
which generally failed.
He was beaten up for good causes
and took it and gave back
in double measure.
We find our way to the language
through him
and through the language
to our questing selves.
Those nights we read till daylight
taught the best secrets,
things like the pride of a good bourbon,
the brave bulls, treachery,
the honor of the tribe.

My Best Guess

So hard to find
the savage child. Window breaker.
Dirt eater. So narrow,
the barefoot path inside.
The fire at the unreachable
center is every hope.
It isn't all there is, but it might be
all that's worth having.
Find out how to be
ragged
and show the world.
Don't worry about angels,
but break open your heart.
Allow everything.
Let everything rise that will.

Modern Romance

She said, "You think you are the master of fire,
but pissing on coals doesn't count.
You're probably not even the master of piss.
I'll bet Jeremy down the street pisses twice as good."

She said, "That wasn't much of a fire, anyway.
Anyone could have doused it with a modest whiz."

She said, "Anyway, I'm cold now.
What are you going to do about it?
Never mind, there's Jeremy."

She wandered off and came back later,
shivering, wet, and stinking of piss.
She said, "Jeremy is a real bastard."

"Yes," he said, with steady nonchalance.
 "Go bathe. We're due at Bingo in an hour."

Please Be Considerate

If you think life is unfair,
consider the horse
you rode in on.

The other guy's horse?
Fuck that horse.

But your horse never
said a bad word
about anybody.

This Particular Second

Sometimes, like now,
I am all wax, no wick.
Sometimes, like now,
I am an undercooked pie.
Sometimes I'm a bullet that misfires,
a duck in the dessert,
a blind man beside naked beauty.
Sometimes I'm a story without syntax.
Sometimes a mystery wound.
Sometimes, like now,
a Roman candle shooting
into my own ear.
Sometimes I'm a swing without a swinger.
Sometimes I'm a ghost that never lived.
A rock thinner than air.
A cure for no disease.
A monkey eating razors.
The world's shortest giraffe.
The tallest bedbug.
The hottest ice cube.
The coldest star.
The saltiest sugar.
The blackest white.
The door nailed shut.
The nails in the flesh.
The horrors of the mind.
The end of the end.
The screaming child in a room full of badgers.
The screaming badger in a room full of nuns.
Sometimes I think I'm fine,
but that's just sometimes.
Just now and then.
Not right now.

The Herd Lined Up

Everyone is in line
for something unknown:
Blue eyes, brown eyes, green, hazel.

The murder of the innocent and the guilty.
Gunshots as common as finger snaps
and more are gone.

Once everyone knew what was right
but truth has been lost under flags,
crosses, and piles of money.

Say it plainly: The liars are evil
and are experts in deception,

but when human blood pools at our feet
will epiphany strike?

The ones in line for slaughter
do not know they are chosen.

Their days are like your day.
They go about their business
just as you do,
or just as your children.

When it is their turn, only some
will be astonished,
though all will unite in terror.

They will be just as you or your children.

None of us know what line we are in.
Not me, not you, not the children.

Manifesto

Who do we write for, if not the people?
The professors and preachers and bosses
don't want or need us.
They are filled with the dogma of the ages.
What use would they have for poetry?
Ask the professors and they will say
they know what poetry is, what it is not
and who is allowed to write it. Fuck them.
Ask the preachers and they will say
the hateful verse of two thousand years past
is plenty to keep us all sated, tithing,
frightened and in line. Fuck them.
Ask the bosses and they will say
they know nothing of poetry
and want to keep it like that
for themselves and also for their workers.
Small minds like small minds and,
even more, the pursuit of money. Fuck them.
But the workers, some of them,
need what we offer,
even if they do not know it.
The same is true for the destitute,
the forgotten, the thrown away.
It is true for young people not yet calcified
by routine and lies.
It is true for the free of spirit,
the seekers, the sad, the lonely, the bright,
the odd, the skulkers in the dark,
the exuberant, the paranoid, the sex fiends,
the drug fiends, the drunks, the mad
and the joyful.
It is true for our beleaguered planet,
being killed minute by minute
by the mindless replication of yesterday.

The people need poetry
even if they do not know it.
Stick to your task, brothers and sisters.
Write new visions.
This is the balm we bring.
This is what holds the light of the world.

Advice to My Children

You must first learn the rules,
and they are taught at dances
and in movie theaters and libraries,
frozen yogurt shops,
walks to class
or strolls through the neighborhood.

They may be fine tuned
over long telephone sessions
with crushes
and giggled conversations
with friends of the heart.

Serious conversations, too.

The rules are flexible,
and some will be yours alone.
They may never be fully grasped,
but you must try.

Sometimes one person or the other
will break them, then decisions
must be made.

Hold hands sometime.
Steal kisses and glances.
Daydream.

Daydreaming
is most important.

Give yourself practice runs
for the real thing,
and also prepare for heartbreak.

Most learn this sooner or later,
and it is debatable which brings less pain.

You will sometimes get discouraged
even in joy. Persevere.

If you have the most excellent luck,
you may find the one.
If you do, love them with all you have.

Be prepared for the long road,
but be ready to let them go,
if you must,
for their own sake.

Love both them and yourself
hard and to the marrow.

Never hide your diamond truth.

An Inadequate Poem for My Children

In the grocery store
and sucker punched
by love.
It stops me cold,
and now it is even hard
to breathe.

But men do not cry
when out in the world,
least of all unshaven
and pushing a shopping cart
down a harshly lighted aisle

heavy with cheeses,
memories of can we get this or that,
and the old, comfortable routine
of Wonder Bread, Twinkies, laughter
and milk.

Incredible Coincidence. Incredible.

The same year God smuggled Tomaz
into a caterpillar (what a funny God Tomaz carries)
I was leaving for Kentucky,
tail tucked and hungover.
It was quite a year. Tomaz knocked balls
out of the park
until he died.
I did not. (Did not die.
Did not knock balls.)

That same year I left Mississippi
there were babies born
who are now living lives of prize winners
flush with laurels — full professors, so bow your head,
grovel —
while Tomaz is dead
and I am mostly
knocked in the balls.

(See what I did there?)

There have been approximately
a great many
women
who have never felt badly
about not knowing I am here.
Same thing goes for readers.
A bunch of them are women, too,
so that changes nothing.

Caterpillars are not so rare,
even if they are the most
nonchalant wizards.
Tomaz still flutters about.

I squint at the mulberry trees, ancient at last,
as Tomaz lights on my cheek,
my thousand faces dancing, blooming,
the very air reciting dreams.

In This Place

I am legion and starving,
beautiful in my flaws
and stupid as a mule.

So, I belong to the dark
which we call
the engine of time.

(Invisible to most, this vast river.)

I belong to the soil,
which we call
the engine of fate.

(Unconsidered and dying.)

I belong to the sky,
which we call
the engine of infinity.

(Incomprehensible, the road to madness.)

I am the living people and the dead.
Give me loaves and fishes,
if you are able.

I belong to confusion,
which we call
the engine of blessing.

I am fat with pride.
and belong to everything.

Every wonder is my flesh.

Hit Parade

We need more songs about poets,
or else we need a world
consumed by flowers.
We need the kind of wind
that takes kites into dark skies
and kites
that don't even need
the wind.
But we really do need
more songs about poets.
What is a kite, after all,
or a wind, beside a sad song
about Kenneth Patchen?
What good, even, are roses?

Hey, Sailor

Less useful than the prostitute,
I compensate
by being more
reasonably
priced.

I admit I am shamed
by flowers,
but my own nectar
is made
of lubricant
words.

Seek me out in the dark,
I beg you.

I will teach how
the moon in eclipse
can be flame,

as delicious
as a stranger's breast, oh,

oh, and as fierce.

Story of My Life

I was born on a
mountaintop
                        dancing. The snap

of twigs
announced
predators and older
children, curious
        about the hubbub.

There should
not have been
panthers,
but what are you
                    going
    to do?

I might return if I'm able.

My bones are scattered
like notes
on a lost piano.

Come springtime,

the flowers
will raise them
up.

The Things We Do for Love

That's the day they screwed
the middle time.
The last time was much later.
The first was only the day before.
Her hair was still golden,
even if it maybe came
from a bottle.
It's always right against time
to pick up the children, isn't it?
School is such a bother.
Tests, tests, tests.
The middle time was the nicest.
Not so much awkward conversation
and rushing.
She had an orgasm, almost.
That last time? Oh, lord.
Who knew when death would come?
They went to the movies
with their spouses after
and all four shared popcorn
from one big tub.
Not everyone wanted the hot butter,
but they compromised,
as they had for years.
But movies are the best,
everyone together in the dark
with their eyes fixed on the world's desire.
They all agreed on that.

From the Get-Go

One hand in the pie and one hand waving,
the fingers all rubbing holes in the flag.
The nation doesn't care,
but it would be nice
if there were pie left for everyone.
One big hand in the pie
and it's curtains for the family
that can't afford shoes
and snow's on the way.
One hand rubbing the eyes
after a weekend drunk.
One hand rubbing soft cotton.
The hands and their promises:
The women in the musky dark
know better.
In case you didn't hear it,
there are double entendres aplenty,
operating like cyphers,
floating in confusion.
Linda and Susie, Molly, Edwina,
Joyce with their shapely despair.
All nighttime raids are suspended
until the body's needs are met.
The bombs will drop later.
The missiles, the grenades,
the poison gas.
The desperate boys, the laughing girls.
Everyone ends in sorrow, you grinning prick.
The body is a funhouse of bent mirrors.
Pleasure is only bait.

Here's My Advice

Buy a book and the world changes.
Don't be a cynic.
Fortunes often turn on small transactions.
Women! Money! Liquor! Drugs! Who knows?
Buy a book and roll the dice.
Maybe you'll get lucky.
Influence can be aces, after all.
I hear sometimes there's sex, but let's not
get all giddy.
This is a good line and that is a good line
and — presto! — you have the illusion
of style.
Day into night never seemed likely,
but keep the faith.
All dark alleys lead somewhere
and poets are so fussy.
The good ones borrow. The best ones steal.
Be a smart thief. See what happens.

What's the Story, Morning Glory?

People awaken in my town and see trees,
their branches jitterbugging
in the blind wind.
Some of them are children
and maybe think innocent thoughts,
and some of them are ancient,
and dumb as fish.
Who are we to question the air?
People awaken in my town and desire sex
but are alone.
Some of them are vile
and some are fine but unlucky,
but none of them are getting any.
People go to work in my town
and sabotage their bosses
or perform heroics without notice.
Someday they will all die.
People awaken in my town
on their last day
without knowing this is it.
They watch the branches
jitterbugging in the wind.
They think their fleeting thoughts.
Some masturbate or pray.
The clever stretch, sigh
and drink their tepid coffee.

Poem for a Dear Lady

I closed my eyes just now (I am very tired
and the road is long)
and saw a clear vision
of Margaret Dalton
as she might have looked fifty years ago,
if fifty years ago she were kind
and beautiful, and filled with the confidence
youth and beauty admit to certain women.
She was dressed in a white blouse
and black pants and gazed at me
with a knowing smile on her unlined face.
Jet black hair.
This was not the Margaret I knew,
old and frightened, mean,
because meanness was what she
was taught by her German father
and the classmates who threw stones.
The Margaret I knew is dead,
besides all else.
But that vision from nowhere.
That smile.
The mystery.

At Your Service

The washing of the feet
as goats bite at the legs
of drunk shepherds
who have mistaken them for sheep.
The glories and the hallelujahs.
The horny housewives
eyeing the horny high school jocks
as the preacher goes on and on.
The goats sing the highest psalms
in their goat language.
(Syntax is problematic.
They are goats, after all.)
The blood on their teeth
embarrasses entire congregation.
The young girls in their new bodies
mouth words to awful hymns
and glow the way they do.
One of them might kill someone
before the day is over,
but never mind.
I have said too much
already.

Driving the Lost Highway

In the car with my poems
hiding somewhere under the seat
or maybe in the glove compartment.
I watch the beautiful sky and say, firmly,
that I wish my poems were here
to see it with me,
hoping to shame them
from being coy.
No dice.
I see an ancient lady who looks like
an Old Testament prophet
and know my poems would love her,
but I don't even try,
because I'm mad at them
and they don't deserve to see her.
Well, more hurt than mad. But still.
I'm in the car with my poems somewhere
and heading down a highway most people
never knew and most others have forgotten.
It's near sunset and the sky is a dying gray,
huge and beautiful.
Strong clouds, majestic birds,
eagles and hawks,
a steady wind.
No more people around and the ancient lady
has gone somewhere she's supposed to,
a pipeline to the mysteries.
I stop trying to lure out my poems
and settle into the drive.
I roll down the windows. I crank the radio.
I sing as hard as I can.
That's when the poems finally come out.
I say hello to them.
They say hello right back.

We sing together as the sun goes down,
off key and glorious.
The stars appear and we sing right out loud.

So, Then?

Within the electric moment
the living things jump
and some glide.

A flash of recognition and then nothing,
but what is gone when nothing can leave?

Within the spark there is sometimes
an acknowledgment of final things.
Therefore, in the beginning was the end.
So simple.

In the end is yesterday, but what comes
before? The electric moment

is the moment of capture.
Still, everything flies if allowed.

Wise minds catch the thunder
between moments of calm,

but we are the odd ones.

You know as well as I do
that everything is swell,
all of it living, burning,
given to us
in the glide.

My Wish

All I ask is to be buried in the rain.
Put me in a gray suit
and close the coffin
and bury me on a rainy day.
Let the mourners be truly sad,
as if some of them loved me.
If one beautiful woman
standing by herself in back
cries silently,
so be it.
Maybe she arrives and leaves alone
and no one knows her name.
All I ask is to be put in the ground
as the rain falls on those who knew me
before they go their separate ways
to get lunch or argue with lovers,
watch a television show,
or simply live the rest of the day
as best they can
and happily forget I was ever here.

It's Just Business

Standard rates apply
and fees are collected
up front.
We feel this is more than fair,
considering the risks we assume.
An arm, a finger, a knee.
These things are negotiable.
Maybe an eye,
if you want to go big
and get it over with.
Maybe an internal organ.
One kidney. A bit of liver.
This is the industry standard,
you understand.
Best practices.
(You can find it in our policy manual,
if you want to take a peek.)
You hesitate, but I don't think
you understand your luck
in dealing with me.
Some of my colleagues
can be very difficult.
Now, tell me all your dreams
and give me your most precious wish.
The hours race by and you are old.
Every beautiful thing
is waiting.

The Night They Raided Minsky's

Oddly alone in this burlesque,
and I am on stage
staring at the floor.
Then the spotlight shines
from somewhere above,
shines directly on me.
The weight of the light is shocking.
The weight of expectation,
which opens me to epiphany:
We are all dead and the world
is made of stone,
or, if this is wrong, there is a possibility
of wood. A possibility of flame.
Oddly alone, though there must be others
somewhere.
Maybe they are watching.
Well, let's give them a show.
Maybe a little song?
Of course, that's not enough.
I know what they want.
Time for me to get undressed,
show my soft, white underbelly,
and start dancing.

Pilgrimage

Even the negatives destroyed now,

aging children posing before stones
to a dead god.

      Jack, what you knew killed
           something
        inside a life
      burning too quick

but still we drove to Lowell
in the snow   Becky standing tragic then me,
captured by click and silver emulsion,
forever thirty in those blurred photographs
which, like us, have faded
      with time.

Jeff Weddle is a poet and writer living in Tuscaloosa, Alabama. He won the Eudora Welty Prize for *Bohemian New Orleans: The Story of the Outsider and Loujon Press* and has also received honors for his fiction and poetry. His work has appeared in Albanian and Spanish translation. Jeff teaches in the School of Library and Information Studies at the University of Alabama.

Also by Jeff Weddle

Vritme Nese Ke Koqe (Kosovo:SabaiumBB, 2023)

How It Went to Pieces (Kung Fu Treachery Press, 2022)

Advice For Cannibals (Poetic Justice Books and Arts, 2021)

There's More to It Than That (Poetic Justice Books and Arts, 2021)

Good Party (Poetic Justice Books and Arts, 2020)

Dead Man's Hand (Poetic Justice Books and Arts, 2019)

A Puncher's Chance (Rust Belt Press, 2019)

Citizen Relent (Unlikely Books, 2019)

It's Colder Than Hell / Starving Elves Eat Reindeer Meat / Santa Claus Is Dead (Alien Buddha Press, 2018)

Heart of the Broken World (Nixes Mate Books, 2017)

Comes to This (Nixes Mate Books, 2017)

When Giraffes Flew (Southern Yellow Pine, 2015)

The Librarian's Guide to Negotiation: Winning Strategies for the Digital Age (co-author, Information Today, 2012)

Betray the Invisible (OEOCO, 2012)

Bohemian New Orleans: The Story of the Outsider and Loujon Press (University Press of Mississippi, 2007)

Acknowledgments

Grateful acknowledgment is made to the following, where some of the poems previously appeared or have been accepted for publication, sometimes in slightly different form or in translation.

Ablueionistas; Alien Buddha Press; Alien Buddha Zine; Beatnik Cowboy; A Compendium of Literary Minds; Country Fried Panda Poets Anthology; Dirty Kids Press; Dumpster Fire Press; Encore; GAS: Poetry, Art & Music; Gasconade Review; Heaven Mail; Heidra; Horror Sleaze Trash; Jimmy Broccoli; Live Nude Poems; Moody Street Irregulars; ObserverKult; Poetry Feast; Raw Art Review; Read Carpet; Rogue Wolf Press; Rust Belt Press; Rye Whiskey Review; Wingnut Brigade; Sacred Chickens; Telegrafi; Wildfire Magazine

Praise for Jeff Weddle

I've translated completely *How It Went to Pieces*. Now I am reading your other books, I will read and re-read and make choices for translation. I hope to be able to publish your book of poetry this spring. I know it will be a hit among poetry lovers. During this year I hope to publish books of Ferlinghetti, Baraka, Corso, Snyder, e. e. cummings and so on. For decades I've been translating their work.

As for your poetry I don't know what I can say, I like it a lot and it reminds me a lot of the Rolling Stones at their best. Which means: simple but strong!

> Fadil Bajraj, Kosovo-based translator and publisher who introduced Beat Generation literature to the Albanian-speaking world. (From a letter to the author)

These poems hit where it hurts and score when it counts. The guy writes like an angel with its hair on fire. End of story.

> John Yamrus, Author of nearly 40 books, the latest being *Twenty Four Poems*.

www.ingramcontent.com/pod-product-compliance
Lightning Source LLC
Chambersburg PA
CBHW032235080426
42735CB00008B/858